T0382005

SLOTHS

James Maclaine

Illustrated by Maribel Lechuga
Additional illustrations by Bonnie Pang
Designed by Claire Morgan and Sam Whibley

Sloth consultant: Professor David Macdonald CBE,
Wildlife Conservation Research Unit, Zoology Department, University of Oxford
Reading consultant: Alison Kelly

Contents

All sloths have three toes on their legs. Their arms have either two or three toes.

Upside down

Sloths live in warm, wet forests in Central and South America.

They hang upside down in trees.

So slow

When sloths move, they're very, very slow.

A sloth lifts just one of its arms when it starts to move.

It grabs a branch before moving its legs across too.

Then the sloth moves its other arm and climbs up slowly.

This sloth is resting on top of a branch.

Sloths sometimes sit in trees instead of hanging.

Even sloths' eyelids move slowly when they blink.

Sloth fur

Sloths have a thick layer of fur under lots of long, shaggy hairs.

This sloth is brushing its fur with its claws.

When sloths hang,
their hairs point down.
This helps rainwater
to drip off.

If you looked closely
at a sloth, you'd spot
lots of moths living
in its fur.

Over 100 moths can be found
on a single sloth.

Turning green

Tiny plants called algae grow in sloths' fur. Algae grow better when it's wet.

In dry weather, the algae in a sloth's fur look brown.

They start to turn green at rainy times each year.

As more algae grow, the sloth gets greener. This helps it to hide from dangerous eagles.

There are lots of algae on this
brown-throated sloth.

When it's dry
again, the algae will fade.

Finding their way

Sloths can't see very well. They use smell and touch so they know where to climb.

A sloth finds its way to the top of a tree to lie in sunlight.

If it gets too hot, the sloth moves in search of shade.

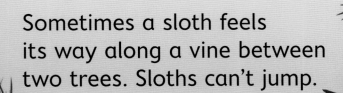

Sometimes a sloth feels its way along a vine between two trees. Sloths can't jump.

This sloth is
bending its neck to
sniff in a different direction.

Three-toed sloths twist their
necks much further than you can.

Going down

Sloths spend very little time on or near the ground.

If a sloth lives by a river, it goes down to drink.

It dangles from roots above the water.

Sloths sometimes move across the forest floor to get to a different tree.

A sloth climbs down a tree trunk bottom first.

When it reaches the ground, it starts to crawl.

It takes the sloth a long time to reach the next tree.

Leaf eaters

Sloths mostly eat leaves, stems and fruit that grow on different trees.

A maned sloth grabs a leafy branch and pulls it to its mouth to eat.

The sloth bites a leaf with its hard lips. Then it uses its teeth to chew and chew.

Two-toed sloths sometimes eat insects and little lizards too.

This brown-throated sloth has found
a tasty, red bud to eat.

Sloth poo

Sloths do poos once a week.

This sloth is pooing next to a tree.

Sloths only do poos on the ground.

The poo is important for the moths that live on sloths.

Female moths leave the sloth to lay their eggs inside its poo.

When the eggs hatch, the baby moths eat the poo.

After growing wings, the young moths fly up to find the sloth.

Sloth fight

Adult sloths live on their own. They try to keep away from other sloths.

An adult male sloth chases any other males that he meets.

As the sloth gets closer, he starts to swipe with his claws.

If the sloths fight, they bite and scratch one another.

These two sloths are wrestling on a branch.

They'll keep fighting until one of them falls to the ground.

Sloths can drop from high up without getting hurt.

Baby sloths

Mother sloths have their babies while hanging from trees. Each mother has only one baby at a time.

When a baby sloth is born, the mother licks it clean.

The baby already has fur and claws. It can open its eyes too.

The baby clings to its mother's tummy and drinks her milk.

This mother sloth's baby is now
two months old.

Growing up

Young sloths stay close to their mothers as they grow up.

This mother sloth is teaching her baby which types of leaves it can eat.

Every young sloth keeps holding onto its mother until it learns how to climb.

At first, it tries to hang by its arms while sitting on its mother.

Then it starts to climb on its own. It will leave its mother after a year.

Strong swimmers

Sloths are surprisingly good at swimming.

Sometimes floods happen where sloths live. Rivers overflow and cover the ground.

To move between trees, a sloth has to swim. First, it climbs into the water.

Then the sloth floats on its tummy. It uses its arms to paddle quickly.

This is a pygmy three-toed sloth.

It's swimming in the sea near a forest.

Baby sloths ride on their mothers' backs in water.

Sloth sounds

Sloths mostly keep quiet, but they can make noises for different reasons.

A sloth hisses at another sloth to tell it to keep away.

If an eagle attacks, a sloth tries to scare it off by growling.

When a female sloth wants to attract male sloths, she makes loud noises.

If a baby sloth falls out of a tree, it calls for its mother.

Meeeeep

Meeeeep

The baby keeps bleating so the mother knows where to find it.

Fast asleep

Sloths sleep for about ten hours every day.

This sloth is leaning back to snooze.

Sloths can hang by their arms and legs even as they sleep.

Sometimes a sleepy sloth curls up into a ball. It rests its head on its chest.

Two-toed sloths climb in between tangles of vines and then fall asleep.

Both three-toed sloths and two-toed sloths are often awake at night.

Glossary

Here are some of the words in this book you might not know. This page tells you what they mean.

 eyelid – a thin fold of skin. Eyelids cover eyes when they're closed.

 claw – a long, sharp nail. Sloths use their claws to hang, climb and fight.

 moth – a type of insect. Some moths live on sloths.

 algae – tiny types of plants. Green algae grow in sloths' fur.

 eagle – a large bird. Some eagles try to catch sloths to eat.

 vine – a type of plant. Vines are long and thin. They grow around trees.

 flood – a very large amount of water. Floods cover dry land.

Usborne Quicklinks

Would you like to find out more about sloths, and watch them climb through the treetops? Visit Usborne Quicklinks for links to websites with videos, facts and activities.

Go to **usborne.com/Quicklinks** and type in the keywords "**beginners sloths**". Make sure you ask a grown-up before going online.

Notes for grown-ups

Please read the internet safety guidelines at Usborne Quicklinks with your child. Children should be supervised online. The websites are regularly reviewed and the links at Usborne Quicklinks are updated. However, Usborne Publishing is not responsible and does not accept liability for the content or availability of any website other than its own.

This pygmy three-toed sloth lives on an island in the Caribbean Sea. Pygmy three-toed sloths can be found nowhere else in the world.

Index

Acknowledgements

Series designer: Helen Edmonds

Photographic manipulation by John Russell

Photo credits

The publishers are grateful to the following for permission to reproduce material:
cover © Michael & Patricia Fogden/Minden Pictures/Alamy Stock Photo; **p.1** © Guy Edwardes Photography/Alamy Stock Photo; **pp.2-3** © Juan Carlos Vindas/Getty Images; **p.5** © Kim Hammar/Alamy Stock Photo; **p.6** © Lukas Kovarik/Alamy Stock Photo; **p.9** © Suzi Eszterhas/Minden Pictures; **p.11** © Blue Planet Archive/Alamy Stock Photo; **p.15** © Juan Carlos Vindas/Getty Images; **p.16** © Suzi Eszterhas/ardea.com; **p.19** © Juan Carlos Vindas/Getty Images; **p.21** © Suzi Eszterhas/naturepl.com; **p.22** © Animals Animals/Animals Animals/SuperStock; **p.25** © Suzi Eszterhas/Minden Pictures/Alamy Stock Photo; **p.28** © Latitude 59 LLP/Alamy Stock Photo; **p.31** © Suzi Eszterhas/Minden Pictures/SuperStock.

Sun, Moon and Stars

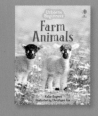
Farm Animals

Elizabeth I

Rubbish & Recycling

Dogs

Horses and ponies

Spiders

Planes

Cats

Ancient Greeks

Volcanoes

Dinosaurs

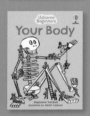
Your Body

Armour

Sharks

The Celts

Vikings

Castles

How flowers grow

Digging up the past

Caterpillars & Butterflies

Weather

Ballet

Tadpoles & Frogs

Pirates

Why do we eat?

Egyptians

Under the Sea

Romans

Eggs & Chicks

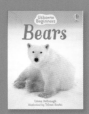
Bears

AZTECS

Trucks

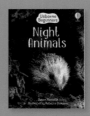
Night Animals

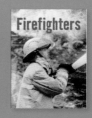
Firefighters

Antarctica

Bugs

COWBOYS

PLANET EARTH

London

Seashore

China

Dangerous Animals

Rainforests

Trees

Reptiles

Ships

Bats

Trains

The Solar System

Knights

Monkeys

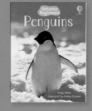
Penguins

Elephants

Tigers

Earthquakes & Tsunamis

Storms and Hurricanes

BEES & WASPS

Wolves

Owls